This Poem ...
Blake Morrison

smith|doorstop

Published 2013 by
smith/doorstop Books
The Poetry Business
Bank Street Arts
32-40 Bank Street
Sheffield S1 2DS

ISBN 978-1-906613-99-0
Typeset by Utter
Printed by People for Print, Sheffield

Acknowledgements

Some of these poems first appeared in *The Guardian, The New
Statesman, The North, Poem, Standpoint, Glits-e,* and *The Liner.*

smith/doorstop Books are a member of Inpress:
www.inpressbooks.co.uk. Distributed by Central Books Ltd.,
99 Wallis Road, London E9 5LN

The Poetry Business is an Arts Council National Portfolio Organisation

Supported by
**ARTS COUNCIL
ENGLAND**

Contents

Caution all prose hogs.
Poetry's a speed bump.
It's there to make you slow down.

Bonus

Time was when poetic talent came dearer than gold ...
– Ovid, *Amores, 3, 8*

This poem is my annual bonus ... I know, I know,
most folk slog away for a modest return with no extras,
and their work's in the public interest,
teaching and healing and cleaning and stuff. Whereas ...

But I'm a poet, and who are you to interfere
if the powers above choose to reward me?
Remember the value of the words I generate
and all I contribute to the cultural economy.

Be warned: if you deprive us poets of our bonuses,
we'll be forced to move and work abroad
in a different language, and London will lose its place
as the poetry hub of the western world.

Is that what you want? No? I thought not.
You're just jealous of the cats that get the cream.
Go on, admit it: we're bloody well worth our bonuses.
Every stanza. Every line-break. Every half-rhyme.

Hacking

This poem has been hacked into.
It was meant to be a private conversation,
the line made secure with end-stops.
But someone cracked the code and listened in.

I hate to think how it will be read
when all I talked about in confidence –
the pizza, the piazza, the back row of the Plaza –
is out there in the open, on the page.

It's not my fault the text went viral
but I feel I've betrayed your trust.
What kind of world are we living in
when poems become public property?

In future I'll keep my texts oblique
so that no one can decrypt them
or discover what I'm driving at
when I speak of the ibis in the rain.

Then my hotline to you will be restored
and you can love me again, as you should:
whoever you are, whatever your name is,
these words are intended just for you.

Super-injuncted

This poem has been super-injuncted.
You're not allowed to read it.
You don't even know that it exists.

A man and a woman meet in a bar,
he a sports star, she a strutting beauty
long and slender as a pheasant's tail.

In his suite, after more drink,
he divides her from her dress
and remainders it on the carpet –

shot silk she feels like as he enters her,
her squared-off, spangly fingernails
leaving stitchwork on his back.

Asleep, he dreams of penalties while she slips
from bed and stands with her cellphone,
pressing keys to remember this

– the premier league cock (shrunk to a walnut),
 the fading letters (Amor Vincit Monica)
in the foliage of his liver-blue tattoo.

'That night was the first of many,'
she will later confide to hacks,
'he was a master of keepy-uppy.'

But the press can't run the story:
the man's good name is on the line,
his happy marriage, his lovely kids,

which is why I've not written this poem
and you're not reading it
and no one even knows that it exists.

This Olympic double acrostic ...

... Is my legacy, a fourteen-tier poem
Bequeathed to the nation, an arena
Left behind for when my race has been run
And the games are officially over.
Kicking on to the finish as we do,
Every poet deserves to be
Memorialised for posterity, whether
Olympian or not. But few who follow will
Remember what we achieved or feel
Regret when we have gone. An obituary
In the paper leaves a mark but only
Sonnets can put us in the record books
Or tell how gamely we struggled to be heard.
No athlete ever practised as hard.

❋

Names count for nothing but the words endure.
Only in sport it's the opposite –
Sprinters and hurdlers say nothing memorable,
It's their times and victories that go on
Record and the beauty of their running that
Remains. Poets should learn from this:
On the page is where we prove ourselves, not in
Media soundbites or performing onstage.
Expression of self is what poetry's for;
Kill the I and you destroy the USP.
Art's more than narcissism, though; great writers
Lose their egos in the act of writing and
By doing so let the reader come alive:
In the mirror of their poems, we find ourselves.

'It Was Good While It Lasted'

This poem is Jimmy Savile's gravestone.
Or was. Given the risk of public outrage
and as a gesture of sympathy to his victims,
it has been removed from the page.

Nor will the exhumation of his body
from the concrete-encased gold coffin
in which it lies at a 45-degree angle facing the sea
be documented in this quatrain.

Whereof we cannot speak except
with prurience, sanctimony or inspired
retrospective wisdom,
thereof we must not say a word.

Obituary

This poem is its own obituary.
At home, quietly, after a short illness.
Beloved son of, mother to, lover of.
Born in obscurity, by a moon river.
Product of the local primary (de la Mare),
then grammar school (Wilfred Owen).
Showed early promise with a metaphor,
the crowning newborn vernixed with ash,
and established a distinctive voice,
that of a fox prowling through London,
but lost direction midway, in a dark wood,
with the mortgage to think of, and the children,
and the distraction of a coffee machine,
before a partial recovery late on, by the coast,
and the cry of terns over the sand dunes,
in blank verse, with a bit of assonance thrown in.
The end itself was disappointing,
as endings always are, a handful of soil
and a hyphen between two dates - no flowers please.

Unspoken

This poem is one I got out of writing.
It's what friends say, after a disaster,
'I suppose you'll get a poem out of this',
because they know what poets are like,
pen in hand as their marriage breaks up
or the curtains close around the coffin.

But this is one I got out of writing:
never got round to, shied away from,
started to draft and then abandoned,
because the words were acid in my throat.

There are things you can say on the page
you would never speak to someone
or even admit to yourself. But this was worse.
This was the gunman in the classroom.
This was the torturer with the pliers.
This was the fire on the 95th floor.

Seminar

'... *if a Sparrow come before my Window, I take part in
its existence and pick about the gravel ...*'
          – Keats, letter to Benjamin Bailey 22 November 1817

This poem is you, sitting in a seminar.
You would like to join in but know nothing about
zones of contestation, problematised binaries,
performativity, generative rupturing
or the ideology of transgressive epistemes.

Luckily others in the seminar do know,
or talk as if they do, or anyway talk.
So you can join the starlings on the telegraph wire,
ride that pushchair with the sleeping toddler,
hide in the blouse of the woman at the bus stop.

Just make sure to be awake, before the end –
nod, applaud, rap your knuckles on the table,
as if you've been enlightened and inspired
and when you leave will see the world afresh,
no longer baffled by its hermeneutics.

Cut

This poem is the director's cut,
several lines longer than the version brought out
last year and with additional features such as
subtitles in German, French and Portugese,
interviews with the four main characters,
and a previously unseen sequence in which the hero appears
to eat his childhood sweetheart (though any viewer of average
intelligence will recognize this as *hommage*).
The poem delights in seeming obscure, even random,
and only slowly does its unifying theme -
about sex, death and the joys of being a cannibal -
rise to the surface, if it can be said to rise at all.
Look out for the scene in which the poet hands a page
of sonnets to the Duchess of Cambridge
so as to cure her of *hyperemesis gravidarum*.
Warning: No adult is allowed to see the poem
(let alone read, recite, copy or burn it)
unless accompanied by a child younger than eight.

Regifting

This poem has been regifted. It was
given me by my cousin, whose aunt
gave it to him last Christmas,
after getting it from me as a birthday present.

There's obviously something wrong
if we all decided to pass on it,
though it's still in its original packaging,
gift-wrapped in the form of a sonnet.

Maybe it's the rhythm, maybe the colour,
maybe the message is too cynical.
Whatever the reason for its lack of allure,

I'll not be the one to break the cycle,
which is why it's here, along with a card,
just for you, reader, with fondest regards.

Call centre

This poem is an automated response system.
To activate it, please slowly speak your name.

I'm sorry but your personality has not been recognised.
Please wait while I transfer you to one of our inoperatives.

Your call is extremely important to us.
Please take a moment to enjoy the silence.

As a valued customer, we'd like to offer you
a special offer open only to new customers.

We are experiencing an unusual volume.
Please keep your voice down.

You now have three options: death from boredom,
death from apoplexy, death by suicide.

Thank you. Your complaint has been referred to our satisfaction unit
where it will be answered with due coarseness.

Energy

This poem is measuring my carbon emissions.
The results are better than yours. Or do I mean worse?
Everyone who emits also omits –
the guilt of consumption is too great.
But I'm working at it, switching off the charm
and cutting down my adjectives.
Already my footprint's more Crusoe than China.
And there's the energy I generate.
Last week, cycling into work,
I made enough kilowatts to light the way home.
Now I'm planning a longer ride, in the Alps.
All I create will go into my saddlebag,
which I'll unbuckle at the finish, before – pouf -
exploding in a brilliant white cloud.

Spikes

This poem is the nearest I came to a medal.
The 800 metres at Senior School.
Two laps of the Top Field, grass not asphalt.
Six lanes marked out, the lime still shiny wet.
Gunby up ahead, uncatchable as ever,
three of us abreast on the last bend, fighting for silver.
I'm in the middle, holding my own,
when Lord veers across, driving me out a lane,
into Proctor. I stumble but keep going for
the line, which we cross together
before collapsing in a heap, nothing between us.
Then I see blood - there are thin red gashes
down my thigh from where I landed behind
the others. Did no one see what happened?
How I was barged? Bastards. Fourth. No medal.
It's only then I feel the spikes, the rake of metal
leaving lanes like the ones we battled
between, except these are marked out in blood.
There are a million worse injustices every day
but that was mine, then, and it still lives with me.

Cane

This poem is the cane I got at school.
What I did to be given it I can't recall

only the head choosing it from the others
where they hung like a rack of billiard cues,

and how he steadied my fingers to make them lie flat,
and studied my palm as though reading it,

and sighed, before the cane swished down. Outside,
my hand squeezed under my armpit, I dreamed

of smuggling the cane home to our greenhouse
to sit in compost, propping the tomatoes,

only stirring when nudged with a watering-can...
Times change. Children today aren't given the cane,

but I've still got mine, beating time like a metronome:
Never did me no harm, never did me no harm.

Birthday

This poem is a toast to my father.
On his ninety-sixth birthday
I fetch the champagne from the fridge
and the fruit cake from the larder,
carry the tray down the corridor,
shove the door open with my shoulder,
set the tray down, straighten the rug,
pull the curtains, light the candles,
fill the champagne flute (last of a set
bought in Switzerland on his honeymoon),
sing Happy Birthday, blow out the candles,
cut the cake, make a wish, and drink to him
and drink and drink till the bottle's empty
twenty-one years after the fact.

Horse

This poem contains traces of horse.
Hoof-parings and saddle sweat and meadow breath.
Amber puffballs of hay-smelling dung.
The hairs on the denim jeans she wore
mucking out the stables and wore again
when we met for a drink, which was why (I told her)
my eyes were watering and my skin had flared up
just as they do with house-dust and cat-hair,
though really it was the letters, J-A-S-O-N,
inked in blue on the back of her hand.

Ah well, I told myself, we can still be friends,
but we didn't meet again after that
and it was only later I learned the truth. Jason!
I see him now, a dapple grey of fifteen hands
and she with her riding crop, half out of the stirrups,
their nostrils flaring and their hearts in tune
as they jump the brush fence to the other side.

Coalition

This poem is a coalition effort.
As we say at every press conference
the Muse and I make a great team.

Between us, we've got everything:
order/inspiration, reason/feeling,
left-side/right-side, etcetera.

Off the record, though,
she's a nightmare to work with -
fails to show when I schedule meetings

then barges in when I'm least expecting it,
and if I remind her who's boss
tells me I'd be lost without her.

New opinion polls suggest
the public have lost faith in us:
I should hang up my laurel wreath,

they say, while my Muse moves on
to someone more dynamic -
a performance poet, say.

We need to sit down together
and come up with a war
epic to restore national pride

or our union will dissolve
in bitterness and name-calling
and a congruence of tears.

Riots

This poem is a riot.
Its letters are hoodies crossing the street,
with valuables looted from Hughes & Co.
Several fires have broken out.
Its stolen metaphors are on CCTV.

Feral, it's been called,
though some blame the parents
and others government cutbacks
and others the television
(which the poem runs off with under its arm).

What it loves is the buzz
of sirens going off
and summer on the skin
and almost getting away with stuff.
Rubber bullets can't stop that

nor six months in the slammer
for stealing bottled water.
Once its sentence is finished
and next August comes round,
the poem plans to riot again.

Inappropriate

This poem is having after-hours drinks.
What a nice dress you're wearing. Is it silk?
No need to slap me! I was only checking the material
you're made of. Shall we carry on talking upstairs?
Suit yourself. I thought you were a girl with ambitions.

This poem is texting pix of sex with its ex.
What's the issue? She's a celeb these days
and celebs love to put themselves about.
You can see what a slut she was. Revenge?
I owe her nothing since she dumped me.

This poem met a sweet young thing backstage.
How young? It didn't ask. You don't, do you,
or didn't then, and she seemed sophisticated,
sucking cock. We're going back 15 years.
She'd be 28 now, by my reckoning.

Avoidance

This poem is an offshore tax haven.
It is sitting under a palm in the Cayman Islands,
Mauritius, Panama, the Seychelles.

You won't find my name on the title page.
A man I've never met became director
by signing as instructed in the box.

The private jetty is reserved for visitors.
Last year my accountant brought his family
to watch the turtles lay their nest-eggs in the sand.

From my balcony there's a view of rusting roofs.
When out cruising I keep to the lower deck.
I'm shy with numbers but reject the word evasive.

A gin and tonic on the terrace sets me up.
Then night falls, swift and heavy, like a trapdoor.
Every island is a man with something to hide.

PM

This poem is David Cameron.

It is rolling up its sleeves
and getting behind our banks.
because we're all in this together.

This poem is rebuilding the future
but we'll all have to make sacrifices
especially the poor and needy.

This poem utterly condemns
the recent sickening scenes
of asylum-seeking and benefit-claiming.

This poem is Tory to the core.
It's the main man, the Head Cam,
the one true Con among the Conmen.

It's David Cameron – vote for me!

Lent

This poem is for Lent – uncluttered
as a freshly cleared draining board,
no one talking and no food on the table,
just the cut-off stalk-ends of a daffodil.

Storm

This poem is a thunderstorm.

First a drum roll, boom-de-de-boom, far off,
and the hubbub of a suitcase over cobbles.

Then a tip-up truck, letting rubble go,
or a fridge rumbling down a rubbish chute.

Then inside the giant's throat: hot breath,
flashing teeth, an IED exploding.

Afterwards cool rain, the leaves running with goodness,
the mending of cracked earth.

FGM

This poem has been genitally mutilated.
It was cut in its infancy, with partial success,
and cut a second time, just now, to finish the job.

The nub has gone and blood's filling the bucket.
Uncut, the poem would have run wild,
instead of lying silent on the page.

There may be pain but it's not like severing a penis.
If God had meant poems to play with themselves
He'd have given them lyres not a saxophone key.

A poem must be clean and neutered.
A poem may give pleasure but can't receive it.
A poem's duty is to honour tradition.

In time the poem will give birth to other poems.
Trimmed and mastered, the poem will be a work of art.

XY

This poem is another bad day for men.
The hunter-gatherers have been at it again.
Three young women kept in a cellar on chains.
A student raped on a bus. An ex with acid thrown
in her face. A wife stabbed on suspicion
of flirting. The bodies of girls as young as nine
found strangled and dumped in a wheelie-bin,
a lay-by, a canal, a country lane.

I look up from the paper to where you sit
with your breakfast – Earl Grey and Greek yoghurt –
and picture the blade going in, or the bullet,
the thing I dread making me complicit
because I can't stop imagining the pain,
and because the killer's chromosomes are mine.

Prism

This poem is a surveillance device.
It is checking your emails, intercepting your calls,
reading your thoughts before you have them.

When that secret you'd not tell to a soul
bobbed past us like a Coke can in the river,
we hoiked it out and stowed it in our files.

All citizens need protecting from themselves.
We've made copies of your intimate photos.
We know the websites you go to for your kicks.

Remember those words you wrote in your cups?
That you thought you'd erased? We found them
in the ether, awaiting transfer to a dropbox:

The empty bird feeders sway in the wind.
There's light through the mesh where the nuts were stored
and the seeds for the goldfinch have all flown.

Exit Interview

This poem is my exit interview.
I'm giving HR my reasons for leaving.
They sit there like psychiatrists, taking notes.

I was happy to begin with, I tell them.
No new arrival could have asked for more:
kindly mentors to help me find my feet,

sleepy afternoons in the sunlit atrium,
a screen and keyboard to disseminate my work.
Records will show that I made good progress,

hit it off with colleagues and line managers
and met the targets I was paid to meet.
What's changed then? No gripe about money or status

just a feeling I've accomplished all I can.
Oh, I know where I'm off to isn't rated,
that no good word has ever been said of it.

But think of the perks. No stress, no deadlines,
no gossip by the water cooler, no sick building syndrome,
no team-building awaydays, no commuter gridlock,

no voicemail, nothing at all for ever and ever –
an unbeatable package, I tell them,
slamming the door behind me as I go.